John Thompson's Modern Course for the Piano — FIFTH GRADE

POPULAR PIANO SOLOS

Pop Hits, Broadway, Movies and More!

Book ISBN-13: 978-1-4234-0908-3
Book/CD ISBN-13: 978-1-4234-1256-4

WILLIS MUSIC

EXCLUSIVELY DISTRIBUTED BY

HAL•LEONARD®
CORPORATION
7777 W. BLUEMOUND RD. P.O. BOX 13819 MILWAUKEE, WI 53213

Visit Hal Leonard Online at
www.halleonard.com

Contents

Cabaret
from the Musical CABARET

Words by Fred Ebb
Music by John Kander
Arranged by Eric Baumgartner

7

Under the Sea
from Walt Disney's THE LITTLE MERMAID

Lyrics by Howard Ashman
Music by Alan Menken
Arranged by Eric Baumgartner

Festively 3/4

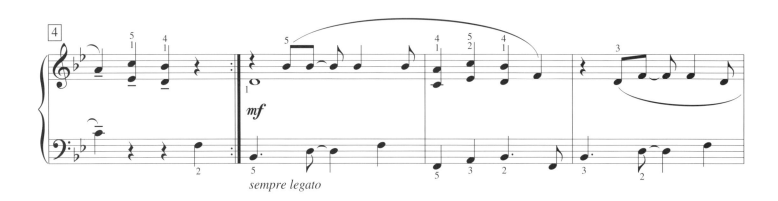

What a Wonderful World

Words and Music by George David Weiss
and Bob Thiele
Arranged by Eric Baumgartner

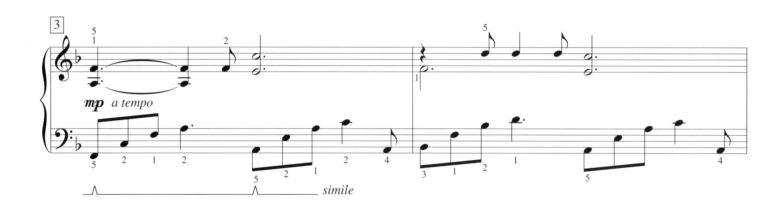

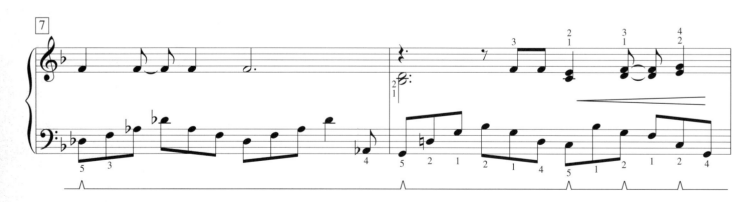

Let It Be

Words and Music by John Lennon
and Paul McCartney
Arranged by Eric Baumgartner

Gently, with a Gospel feel

Puttin' On the Ritz
from the Motion Picture PUTTIN' ON THE RITZ

Words and Music by
Irving Berlin
Arranged by Eric Baumgartner

Très sophistiqué

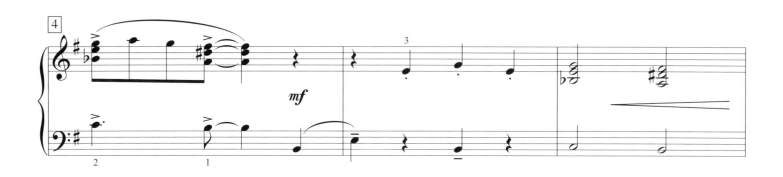

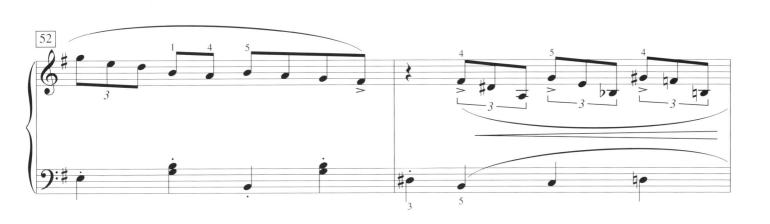

D.S. al Coda

CODA

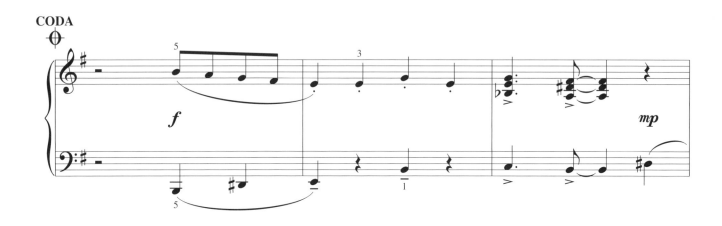

In the Mood

By Joe Garland
Arranged by Eric Baumgartner

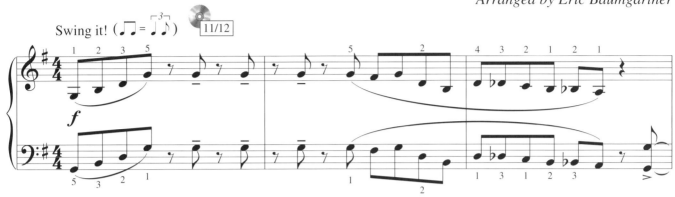

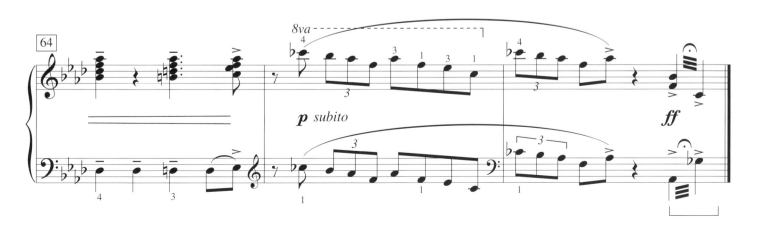

Be Our Guest
from Walt Disney's BEAUTY AND THE BEAST

Lyrics by Howard Ashman
Music by Alan Menken
Arranged by Eric Baumgartner

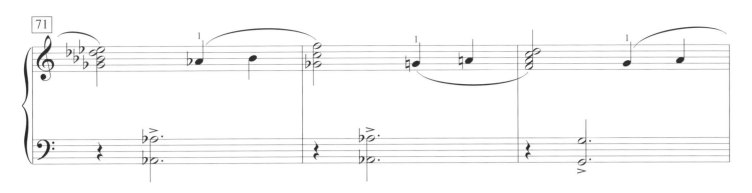

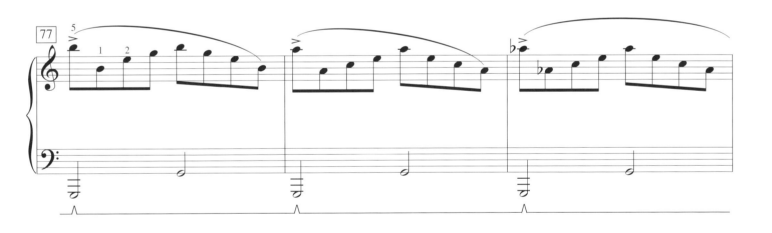

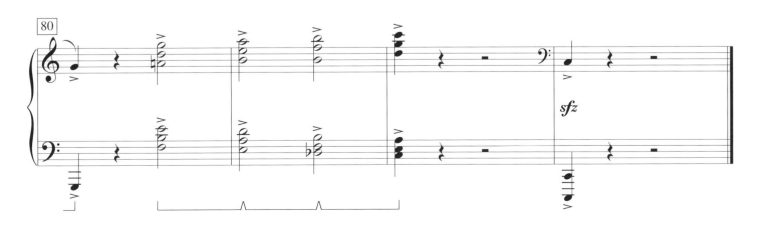

Georgia on My Mind

Words by Stuart Gorrell
Music by Hoagy Carmichael
Arranged by Eric Baumgartner

(continue pedal judiciously!)

Playfully (slightly faster)

detached (no pedal)

Linus and Lucy

By Vince Guaraldi
Arranged by Eric Baumgartner

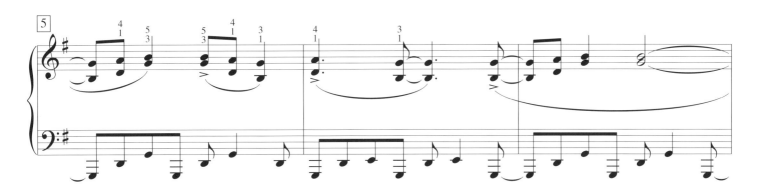

The Way You Look Tonight
from SWING TIME

Words by Dorothy Fields
Music by Jerome Kern
Arranged by Eric Baumgartner

Freely, with great warmth 19/20

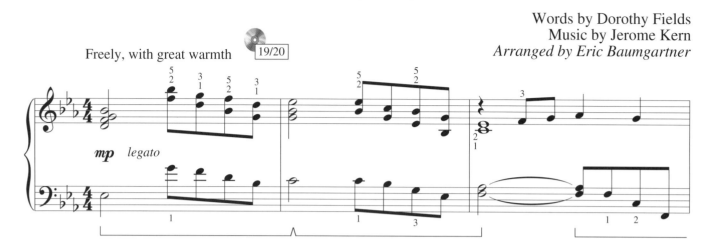

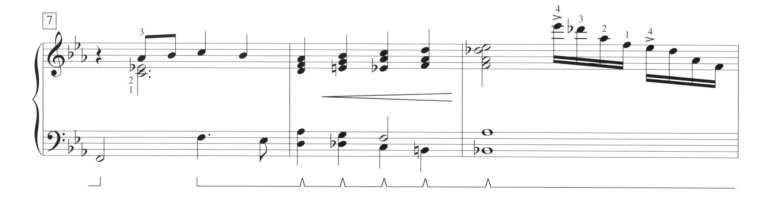

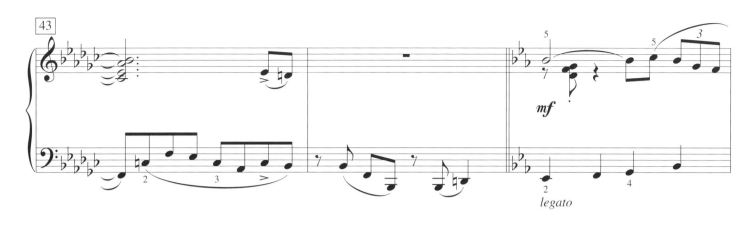

48

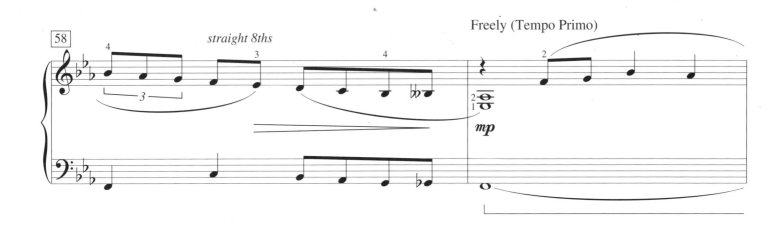

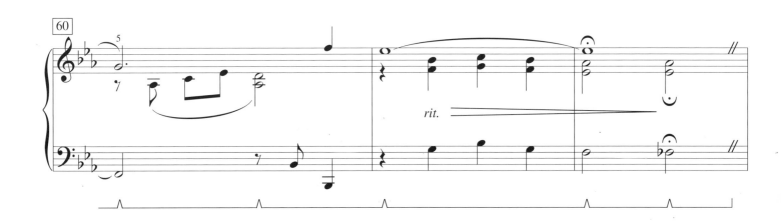